S0-ABR-962

GROWING-POINTS

Growing-Points

new poems by

Elizabeth Jennings

Dufour Editions, Inc.

For O. B.

Acknowledgements are due to the editors of the following periodicals in which some of these poems first appeared: *Critical Quarterly, New Statesman, The New York Times, Meridian, Poetry* (USA), *The Tablet, Sunday Times, Wave, Poetry Nation, The Scotsman, Cornhill,* and *Southern Arts.*

ISBN 8023 1262 4
LC Number 75–7932

First published in the United States in 1975
by Dufour Editions, Inc., Chester Springs,
Pennsylvania, 19425.

Printed in Great Britain by W & J Mackay Limited, Chatham

4

CONTENTS

BEECH

They will not go. These leaves insist on staying.
Coinage like theirs looked frail six weeks ago.
What hintings at, excitement of delaying,
Almost as if some richer fruits could grow

If leaves hung on against each swipe of storm,
If branches bent but still did not give way.
Today is brushed with sun. The leaves are warm.
I picked one from the pavement and it lay

With borrowed shining on my Winter hand.
Persistence of this nature sends the pulse
Beating more rapidly. When will it end,

That pride of leaves? When will the branches be
Utterly bare, and seem like something else,
Now half-forgotten, no part of a tree?

GROWING

Not to be passive simply, never that.
Watchful, yes, but wondering. It seems
Strange, your world, and must do always, yet
Haven't you often been caught out in dreams

And changed your terms of reference, escaped
From the long rummaging with words, with things,
Then found the very purpose that you mapped
Has moved? The poem leaves you and it sings.

And you have changed. Your whispered world is not
Yours any longer. It's not there you grow.
I tell you that your flowers will find no plot

Except when you have left them free and slow,
While you attend to other things. Do not
Tamper with touching. Others pick, you know.

TRANSFORMATION

Always I trip myself up when I try
To plan exactly what I'll say to you.
I should allow for how my feelings lie
Ready to leap up, showing what is true,

But in a way I never had designed.
How is it you are always ready when
Those linked ideas like beads within my mind
Break from their thread and scatter tears again?

I am amazed, and distances depart,
Words touch me back to quiet. I am free
Who could not guess such misery would start

And stop so quickly, change the afternoon
And, far much more than that, transfigure me.
Trusting myself, I enter night, stars, moon.

TO THE CORE

You have tried so hard to reach the core
Of what you tell us that you think you are.
Friends find you out, mirrors now explore,
Or you yourself, both eyes gripped to a star

Or two defensive eyes you can't stare out,
Feel down your flesh, with careful fingers, thin
As worn-out thoughts, and find the scars of doubt.
You test appearances upon your skin.

Truth tastes strange to you and lips learn warnings.
Are you afraid when you reach out and kiss
The air, your breath accepting every morning's

Terrible trust? We learn all fear in ways
No books describe to us. We must dismiss
All but the ghosts which give back our own gaze.

A QUARTET

Four people in a street where houses were
Devoted to their silence. Voices went
Into an argument. The other pair
Looked at each other with a quiet assent.

So speech, so echoes. What were we explaining?
Pitting ourselves against the stars perhaps?
Two did not move, or need a breath-regaining.
Pause meant a stir of love, for us a lapse

In thought. There was no feeling in our speech
Except the easing out to victory.
Tempers were kept. Better if we had each

Been silent, let the other two go off.
There was one lamp disputing with a tree.
Ideas of ours broke through those looks of love.

RHETORIC

He told us that it mattered how a bird
(Not naming it) should have its wings so taut
That it was watchful always, could be stirred
By all events except the being caught

And caged by us. Bright symbols bubbled then
Out of his mouth, poets handed lines
To prove his feelings. Quiet once again,
He gave me territory, gave me signs.

The need to prove had gone now for a time,
Yet I was not at ease, was shouldered out,
First by the echoes of a verse or rhyme,

Then by these people's quiet dexterity.
I had no need of birds to show my doubt
But searched the night for some simplicity.

TRANCE

Naked as possible in cities, these
Young look enchanted. Each attentive face
Could shine a god or goddess in the trees
Of a great forest where the roots found place

Long before man. Yes, in this daze of heat,
Stripped bodies could have stepped from anywhere
To anywhere. The street's no more a street
Of houses where the people have to share

The sense of time. Look, naked children run
Into the water, splashing fountains too
Constant for usual days. They have begun

To change before the watchers' eyes and show
How light is palpable, how day is new,
And, strangely, more so in the sunset glow.

IN A GARDEN

When the gardener has gone this garden
Looks wistful and seems waiting an event.
It is so spruce, a metaphor of Eden
And even more so since the gardener went,

Quietly godlike, but, of course, he had
Not made me promise anything, and I
Had no one tempting me to make the bad
Choice. Yet I still felt lost and wonder why.

Even the beech tree from next door which shares
Its shadow with me, seemed a kind of threat.
Everything was too neat and someone cares

In the wrong way. I need not have stood long
Mocked by the smell of a mown lawn, and yet
I did. Sickness for Eden was so strong.

GRAPES

Those grapes, ready for picking, are the sign
Of harvest and of Sacrament. Do not
Touch them; wait for the ones who tread the wine,
See Southern air surround that bunch, that knot

Of juice held in. In Winter vines appear
Pitiful as a scarecrow. No one would
Guess from their crippled and reluctant air
That such refreshment, such fermenting could

Come from what seem dry bones left after death.
But, look now, how those pregnant bunches hang,
Swinging upon a pendulum of breath,

Intense small globes of purple till the hour
Of expert clipping comes. There is a pang
In seeing so much fullness change its power.

AMONG STRANGERS

Changed by the darkness their indifference shed
Can you be undiminished yet and share
The harmony you find in picture, bed,
In that defiant moth that meets the air

And passes through it and flies on? Can you
Find in the punishings of this no-love
Yourself, the bell your mind which still rings true
As you face what must be well-known enough?

Back to your childhood, are you now before
Any demands? You were not powerless though,
You cried your need out, joining others. Why

Do you divide and count the distance so?
Look, they are harmless and you need not try
To prise their difference open any more.

THE QUALITY OF GOODNESS

Brought up perhaps on some quiet wave of sea
When the boat vanishes and surf reclines
And seen from close at hand as suddenly
A figure folded on the sand's designs

And rising, moving inland—so you stare
With a compassionate serenity
And gaze into my moment of despair.
Total decorum and simplicity.

So I survive and step upon the shore
Which you have yielded. No demands are made.
My laughter is not false, there is no more

Deception. I look back at you, return
Your gaze, am calm upon those tide-out sands,
Sea heard and smelt, too distant to discern.

NO REST

Even while I sit and think and see
Patterns around me which my eyes arrange,
Even while battling out of poetry,
I know some rising in me, summon change

And am existing out of literature,
Not among words or papers any more
But moving among freedoms that are pure.
O no I am not artist but restore

All that was there already, only needing
A touch here; I correct but not improve.
Or change the metaphor—say I am weeding

A garden planted on a stair-cased hill.
I climb and pluck and everywhere I move
I feel unsettled but am learning skill.

FOR THE MIND EXPLORERS

What have you done to some of us privately, to perhaps all publicly
                                                    since you have
Taken away our fables, a child's toys, taken and hidden, sometimes
                                                    destroyed them,
 Or so it seems, "for our good". What is this "good" that comes
                                                    with no nurses
That a language, a tongue or one imagination require? You have lived,
                                                    acted, written, some of you even
 Have prophesied, have thus taken over our old role while we stand,
                                                    gagged, hands tied, in a small cell.
But not for long. We see to that, we confound you by admitting
                                                    you, by letting you

 Trespass upon preserves poets once thought theirs alone. We do more,
We grant you a dispensation to take away our symbols, but in our
                                                    wakeful nights, since you have now
 Taken away at least some of our dreams, we are gentle with you,
                                                    own you and like the
Raiders, but not spoilers, we have always been, we have plundered,
                                                    your found, held coins and
 With extreme delicacy, been Midas with what you have done, said
                                                    or thought. So our magnanimity must
Admit its debt to you—no war, no rage, no guilt, only now gratitude
                                                    and a gentleness.

19

THUNDER AND A BOY

(for T.)

That great bubble of silence, almost tangible quiet was shattered.
There was no prelude, the huge chord
Broke and sounded timpani over the town, and then lightning, first
darting, then strong bar
Taking hold of the sky, taking hold of us as we sank into primitive
people
Wondering at and frightened of the elements, forgetting so swiftly
how naming had once seemed
To give them into our hands. Not any longer. We were powerless
now completely

But today we have risen with the rain and, though it is torrential,
we believe at moments that we
Still have power over that. We are wrong. Those birds escaping
through showers show us
They are more imperial than we are. We shift, talk, doze, look at
papers
Though one child is remembering how last night he stood with defiance

And joy at his window and shouted, "Do it again, God, do it again!"
Can we say he was less wise than us? We cannot. He acknowledged
Zeus
Thor, God the Father, and was prepared to cheer or dispute with any
of them
This afternoon he watches the sky, praying the night will show God's
strength again
And he, without fear, feel those drums beating and bursting through
his defended, invisible mind.

20

FRESHNESS

Good, yes, good, gracious and giving a feeling of
Redemption, is redemption—I mean this open strewn-before-you
                                   liberty of
Knowing small kindnesses deeply. It is like going into those libraries
                                where chained
Books are and, forgetting there is a custodian, librarian, it does not
                                    matter.
You see an illustration, a story from the Bible or an old fable twined
                                    round
One letter. It is like that—this awareness of warmth and also returning
                                       it.

The Alphabet is being learnt again, it is new and amazing when you
                                  see such
Strange Arabic shapes forming words, telling feelings, assisting,
                                  triumphing.
You read and you understand as deeply as you do these faces,
More deeply. You respond and are illuminated and radiant yourself,
Finding friendship so unexpectedly, yet so, when acknowledged,
Fitting, in or out of a time sequence, by a need, a renewal, a victory.

A QUIET ENEMY

Never doubting, he goes on with a routine of perpetual
Small destructions. It would be childlike were there not, behind the
thick grin, a
Masterly malice, acquired quickly and willingly so that all others who
Move where he is must either learn an even swifter immunity or else
Put on a thin mask, say polite words fast, then run, themselves now
Committed to childhood, to that fear which was generated in grates
Of nurseries or back-rooms. "You should not be sensitive"

Others mock, others who do not align themselves with this youth
but can bear,
Even laugh away afterwards, the assurance that his smile will end, if
not begin
With a malice you cannot compete with, nor wish to, ever, for
There is power to hurt here and you crave protection. Is there anyone
strong enough,
Flexible enough to uphold your cause? It seems doubtful for he will
at once
Have their prowess recognised, know they are prepared and so hand a
quick draft
Of a treaty of courtesy. You, meanwhile, wait for what is, after all,
his war to break out again, at any time, any.

I FEEL

I feel I could be turned to ice
If this goes on, if this goes on.
I feel I could be buried twice
And still the death not yet be done.

I feel I could be turned to fire
If there can be no end to this.
I know within me such desire
No kiss could satisfy, no kiss.

I feel I could be turned to stone,
A solid block not carved at all,
Because I feel so much alone.
I could be grave-stone or a wall.

But better to be turned to earth
Where other things at least can grow.
I could be then a part of birth,
Passive, not knowing how to know.

BIRD STUDY

A worm writhes and you have some power
Of knowing when and where to strike.
Then suddenly bread in a shower.
Being a bird is like

This and a feathered overcoat,
A throb of sound, a balanced wing,
A quiver of the beak and throat,
A gossip-mongering.

But higher up a hawk will take
Stature of stars, a comet-fall,
Or else a swan that oars a lake,
Or one note could be all.

I am obsessed with energy
I never touch. I am alive
To what I only hear and see,
The sweep, the sharp, the drive.

TOWARDS A RELIGIOUS POEM

Decrees of a dead tongue gone,
The flicker of Greek in the vernacular,
An age for the East and Yoga,
For lotus and resting. One word
Cannot be spoken or carved.
If music suggests it, it erred.
Christ in this age you are nameless,
Your praises and slanders have sunk
To oaths. Love has somehow slipped by
What once throbbed in an occupied sky.

In my stanzas I'll only allow
The silence of a tripped tongue,
The concerns and cries of creation
To hold you, as always, but more now.
The Prophets and all their books prosper,
But here as a Christmas comes closer,
Awe will be speechless, and magic
Be dropped like an acrobat's pitfall.
The absence, the emptiness echo,
A girl with a cradle to borrow.

AFTER A TIME
(for a friend dead two years)

I have not stood at this grave nor have I
Been where men come at last to silence when
Death sends them to instinctive ceremony,
Whether in torturing sun or fitting rain,
Whether they stare or cry.

What do I say who never put a wreath
Down for a father or this friend? Someone
Will make the speech for me. O this dear death,
Two years of missing all have been undone,
Yet I am growing with

Spontaneous strengths, blessings I did not claim—
Laughter, a child, knowledge of justice and
Faith like a cross which oddly bears my name,
Falls round my neck. In early hours I stand
Reflecting how I came

To this. What takes me through the corridors
Of grief? Was it the touch of love, that leading thread
Which drew me to glad grief from wrong remorse,
Wiped off the dust and let me see the dead
With new care now, new laws?

THE LORD'S PRAYER

"Give us this day." Give us this day and night.
Give us the bread, the sky. Give us the power
To bend and not be broken by your light.

And let us soothe and sway like the new flower
Which closes, opens to the night, the day,
Which stretches up and rides upon a power

More than its own, whose freedom is the play
Of light, for whom the earth and air are bread.
Give us the shorter night, the longer day.

In thirty years so many words were spread,
And miracles. An undefeated death
Has passed as Easter passed, but those words said

Finger our doubt and run along our breath.

MEDITATION ON THE NATIVITY

All gods and goddesses, all looked up to
And argued with and threatened. All that fear
Which man shows to the very old and new—
All this, all these have gone. They disappear
In fables coming true,

In acts so simple that we are amazed—
A woman and a child. He trusts, she soothes.
Men see serenity and they are pleased.
Placating prophets talked but here are truths
All men have only praised

Before in dreams. Lost legends here are pressed
Not on to paper but in flesh and blood,
A promise kept. Her modesties divest
Our guilt of shame as she hands him her food
And he smiles on her breast.

Painters' perceptions, visionaries' long
Torments and silence, blossom here and speak.
Listen, our murmurs are a cradle-song,
Look, we are found who seldom dared to seek—
A maid, a child, God young.

CHRIST ON THE CROSS

Forgive them, Father, forgive them Father who
Is in my heart. How frightened she who stands,
My mother with my friend. The soldiers too,
Help me forgive them who have nailed my hands.
It seems so long ago

I talked in Temples. O the streams where John,
Another, poured the fountain on my head.
Father, I tell my mother that a son,
My friend, shall care for her when I am dead.
I am so dizzy on

This wood. The waters flow but now from me.
I have been chosen. Father, I am you
Who breathed, then sapped the great man-offered tree.
Spirit within me, there are risings too.
Father, forgive now, me.

LENT BEGINNING 1974

This is the beginning of it. Towards
The torn hill, through the ash of earth
We stumble, gathering our words
From staring death, blind birth.

And what round many necks hangs now
As charm, still casts its shadow of
Shame like the noose upon that bough,
The burdenings of love.

Believe or not—we are all kin
When violence sweats out as blood,
When dared compassions smile at sin,
One cruel thought stuns to good.

EASTER DUTIES

They are called duties. People must confess,
Through garlic-smelling grilles or in quiet rooms,
All the year's mis-events—unhelped distress,
Griefs lingered over, *accidie* in dreams,
And hear the words which bless

And unbind, eat the bread and feel the cross
Hurting only a little, hinting more.
Why do I feel, in all these acts, a loss,
As if a marvel I had waited for
Were a cheap toy to toss

Away, the giver gone? Why do I care
In this uncaring? I need gods on earth,
The wonder felt, sleep which I somehow share
Because it is a going back to birth.
And, yes, I want to bear

Anticipated laughter, jokes which once
Meant calibre and bite but did not make
Anyone sad. Prayer yet could be a dance
But still a cross. I offer small heartbreak,
Catch grace almost by chance.

WHITSUN SACRAMENT

Others anoint you but you choose your own name.
This comes with childhood just about to leave.
It comes with new self-consciousness, old shame,
Arrives when we are not sure we believe.
We read about a flame

And answers when we question every word,
Mumble our motives. Spirit, Spirit, where
Are you to be caught now and where be heard?
We only feel the pitched-low, taunting air.
There was talk of a bird,

A dove. Where is peace now in our unrest—
The childish questions in the throbbing mind,
The new name, itching loins, the shaping breast?
When we most need a tongue we only find
Christ at his silentest.

OUT OF THE HEIGHTS

Out of the preening and impetuous heights
Where we look down and do not fear and risk
The snow escaping, the ice-melting flights,

And where we spin the sun a golden disc
And do not care and watch the clouds attend
The tall sky's dazzling and arched arabesque,

Out of those places where we think we end
Unhappiness, catch love within a final hand,
God, from such places keep us and defend

The innocence we do not understand,
The darknesses to which we must descend.

THE NATURE OF PRAYER
(a debt to Van Gogh's "Crooked Church")

Maybe a mad fit made you set it there
Askew, bent to the wind, the blue-print gone
Awry, or did it? Isn't every prayer
We say oblique, unsure, seldom a simple one,
Shaken as your stone tightening in the air?

Decorum smiles a little. Columns, domes
Are sights, are aspirations. We can't dwell
For long among such loftiness. Our homes
Of prayer are shaky and, yes, parts of Hell
Fragment the depths from which the great cry comes.

THOMAS AQUINAS

Thinking incessantly, making cogitations always but as keenly,
                                        freshly as the child
He had been who asked repeatedly "What is God?" and was pursued
                                by this inquiry till grown-up,
And family factions argued, as they thought logically, that he
Must be an Abbot, they had long doomed this—he, Thomas of Aquin,
                                then revolted, but typically
Mildly and unviolently. No aristocracy for him but in ideas and he
                                had settled his destiny to be
A Dominican friar. The one act of outrage we know of is when
Relations sent in women to tempt his body and he drove them out
                                                    with a

Burning brand. After that, Albert to instruct him, Plato read and
                                        discarded, then
Aristotle transformed with clarity into a great system coinciding with
                                                    every
Christian dogma, dancing metaphysical thought, and he put down
                                calmly the ending in
The Summa for students, for others more and deeper, if possible,
                                                matters.
And he, who patterned and explained the world, dined with Louis of
                                            France, still
Stayed the child of great questions, saint but like an angel, and rightly,
                                                        now
Known among us as the Angelic Doctor, a Church's title for one
        whose sole wish was for the pure gold of continual inquiry.

They fall in easy poses as if they
   Knew the sun's moods by heart,
Expected it, as in hot lands. Each day
   They soon become a part

Of the stretched grass unmown where shining flowers
   Stare straight into the light.
Grown-ups and children all accept its powers
   As if it were a right.

They are adaptable to changes, so
   Here where the sun can bruise
With brightness where they bask, they all still know
   This climate is for use.

Yet they are not complacent. Watch them run
   Fast when the sun comes out
And for a moment shrug fore-knowledge. Sun
   Is strong before all doubt.

IN A PICTURE GALLERY

Show me a gallery of air
And walls shored up with paintings through
Which we can climb. A step, a stair
Takes us to sunsets or a view
Of light sufficient to a square
Of harlequinning people who

Set minds to music. Do you hear
A murmur of continued flight?
Paint, sound and word are everywhere,
A quick kaleidoscope of light.
Are paintings far or are we near
This texture of, this sound of sight?

MONDRIAN

Attempt a parody of this:
Prepare the paints, make measurements,
Keep an eye cocked on memory,
Call up geometry, stand back,
Extend the rainbow's ready scope.

But Mondrian will not appear.
He starves still with an easel too
Heavy to hang on, fever high,
Caught too late with canvases
For barter in the auction rooms.

Can abstractions tell the tale?
Are portraits put in angles, squares?
Still life, still death and one thing more—
The dignity of distances,
The lofty white a man's last breath.

REMBRANDT'S LATE SELF-PORTRAITS

You are confronted with yourself. Each year
The pouches fill, the skin is uglier.
You give it all unflinchingly. You stare
Into yourself, beyond. Your brush's care
Runs with self-knowledge. Here

Is a humility at one with craft.
There is no arrogance. Pride is apart
From this self-scrutiny. You make light drift
The way you want. Your face is bruised and hurt
But there is still love left.

Love of the art and others. To the last
Experiment went on. You stared beyond
Your age, the times. You also plucked the past
And tempered it. Self-portraits understand,
And old age can divest,

With truthful changes, us of fear of death.
Look, a new anguish. There, the bloated nose,
The sadness and the joy. To paint's to breathe,
And all the darknesses are dared. You chose
What each must reckon with.

MOZART'S HORN CONCERTOS

Not for war or hunting cry
Is this; it gentles down the heart
So there's no question asking "Why

Does man exist?" God gave him art,
And God is proved in every note
And every sound takes its own part

In what a young composer wrote
Who ended in a pauper's grave.
The disc is on, the patterns float

And I feel back at some strange start
And marvel at what Mozart gave.

A SCHOLAR EMPEROR OF THE TANG DYNASTY

Dazzling it was indeed, a golden age,
The lakes ran round the palaces, the park
Was, yes, a turned, illuminated page.
   You did not think of dark

Or only as a time when candles curled
Over a manuscript and filled the air
With pens, with eyes to circumscribe the world,
   And you were moving there,

No autocrat but patron till a strong
And swarming dynasty took off your power,
Put you in exile. Poetry, the long
   Finger of time, its hour,

Gave you the diffidence and dared you look
At moon-extending shadows, short-lived sun.
You also added letters to a book
   But now a home-sick one.

Wasn't it worth it? Didn't all those days
Of letting others write and paint allow
This gift of loss, lament which felt like praise
   And proves it is so now?

41

WONDER
(Homage to Wallace Stevens)

Wonder exerts itself now as the sky
Holds back a crescent moon, contains the stars.
So we are painters of a yesterday
Cold and decisive. We are feverish
With meditations of a Winter Law
Though Spring was brandished at us for a day.

Citizens of climate we depend
Not on the comfortable clock, the warm
Cry of a morning song, but on the shape
Of hope, the heralding imagination,
The sanguine making and the lonely rites
We exercise in space we leave alone.

Prophets may preside and they will choose
Clouds for a throne. The background to their speech
Will be those fiery peaks a painter gives
As a composer shares an interval,
As poet pauses, holding sound away
From wood, as worshippers draw back from gods.

A CHINESE SAGE

A Chinese sage once took every word distilled, altered and
                                                    perfected
In private till for him it seemed a poem, yes he took this to a peasant
                                                    woman,
Read it to her softly and slowly and waited for her rough-voiced
                                                    assurance that
Certain words she could understand, others were meaningless to her.
                                                    Very discreetly
But decisively, and with no arguments, this sage crossed out every
                                                    word that was foreign to
A woman of simplicity who knew labours of the soil and the house,
                                                    who had no
Dealings other than this with poetry, art of any kind, yet by his

Magnanimity, more, his humility, became his mentor, guided him
Out of all obscurity, not with wearying argument or even quiet
                                                    coaxing, but by the fact
That she was a world he could only enter through her. Hay, beds,
                                                    crude meals, lust
Subdued his wit, bodied out his verse, cancelled cleverness. And, I ask,
                                                    was he
Most poet or most philosopher in this uncrowned wisdom, writing
In the reign of Charlemagne, paring simplicities to a peace no
                    Emperor was ever enticed by or even dreamed of?

43

ELEGY FOR W. H. AUDEN

Stones endure as your first and last things.
The carpet slippers, the leather skin,
The incorrigible laughter inaccurately aped,

Those late epigrams which obviously were
The acute desperation of that laughter—
These are forgotten almost already.

But the stone your student hand held gently,
Schoolboy hair flopped over years later,
The limestone which reminded you of love

And caught the last strains of your lyrical perceptions,
The walks out of Italy into Austria,
All that grey North which you set glowing—

Yes, it is geology, quarries and tools,
The precise tap on the finished fossil,
And last the shuffle on Christ Church cobbles,

The cobbles you must have stared at rather
Than look up as Wren's Tom trembled your hours—
All these are a life you refused to surrender.

No glass-cases and no museums.
All your grand operas opened into caves
Where your Orators shout and your Mirror is shining.

The Sea stands still but your landscape moves.

44

PROSPERO

All back into their places, steps
Printed on sand, and air to air
Confides, great fruit from spent trees drops.
O Prospero, how you prepare

And ravish in the giving back,
Lamb to the ewe, isle to the sea
And Ariel self-swung and quick
In that good hour of setting free.

We know now how long that language,
Your language, had been dancing in you but
  Suppressed, held back by hard work, the debt
You owed to discipline. But no one, not one
  Stopped you looking, dissecting at a glance
A leaf, a tree's stump, while in your mind
  The long thought-over, now fermented
Ideas of Duns Scotus were waiting, the vintage
  Years about to be bottled at one sign, a word
From a Superior about the wreck you had read of.
  Worked-out ideas, your "instress" and "inscape",
Problems of prosody, "Sprung Rhythm", came out dancing,
  Linked with that subject, and you wrote at last

Guiltless, no squabble now between your vocation,
Endurance chosen as a priest, with art, two arts
  Now stretching within you with all the force of
Deliberations held back. And the discipline itself
  Appeared in selected stanzas, half-rhymes, senses once subdued
Unleashed into another order. A nun, a shipwreck
  Were set down, had happened but now would happen
Over and over in the committed, inexorable, also defenceless
  Way in which poems are always vulnerable. And every long look
At a leaf's individuality or the mark, his own, on a man's face
  Was dynamic. And the heroism heard of
Found place with all your admirations, while God's Presence
  Was granted a new kind of immanence in your lines. Doubtless

The no-understanding of others hurt but, far deeper
  And like the sea you wrote of, the fitness,
Inexorably of this exercise and joy, flowered in you, jetsam
  To others in time, acknowledged by you and by us
Years later. Let us hope you had some inkling of this
  As you rode through so many other poems until Dublin
Felled you like an axe or a wave into
  A desirable death, your work around you
Careful as carved stones simply waiting to be picked up,
  Wondered at, not static but dynamically precious,
Named by you, found by us, never diminishing.

46

PERFORMER

Tight-roper, care, do not look down,
Think of the thread beneath your foot,
Forget the pony and the clown,
Discard the circus, see before
Your gaze a safety held, complete
And, after that, the tidal roar

Of watchers, some of whom no doubt
Wanted a death. You have an hour
When you can cast your terror out,
Depend no more on balance but
On earth whose ground gives you the power,
You think, to snatch that rope and cut.

A PLAY AT AVIGNON

Emptiness after midnight since the voices
Had stopped at last, no echo left behind
   Within that courtyard. Stars had crowded out
Sound, and because there had been voices once
   There was a vacancy that almost, now,
Seemed to be measurable. The actors had
   Spoken their classic lines and simply bowed
And moved from sight. Day would redeem the view,
   The famous broken bridge turn thoughts to rivers
Or else to painting. Southern atmosphere,
   Pervasive and imprisoning, would return

And pick each small square out, each watered field,
Light point the way to Orange or to Nîmes,
   And all Provence be like a text of which
You know the language, linger on the page
   And hear the voices speaking in your mind
Different from those within the palace of
   Disputed Popes. So Avignon arranges
Itself and seen from any point you choose,
   Softens and ripens as the day proceeds
Never preparing you but letting happen
   Those voices, the whole city slipped from sight.

OPERA

These lovers must rely
On the adjustment of the wood and strings
Which, in their turn, are guided by
    The baton beating down the air.
Italian, French or German rings
Towards the fatal hour. The theatre

Is words subjected to
The stretch and fling of sound. Poets withdraw
Or let their rhythms here subdue
    Themselves. Meanings also demur
Without poetic justice, law.
Yet it is this subjection that can stir

Us by a story which
Climbs out of farce into high tragedy,
Love thrives upon the rich
    Deceptions winnowing the ear,
While instruments and voices free
Us to rejoicing pain and apt despair.

AFTER A PLAY

The wind in spasms swept the street
As we walked very quietly
Till cold and silence seemed to meet
And make one point—one star set free
Between two stormy clouds. We leant
Upon both wind and words we meant.

A tense and joyful audience had
Thronged in the theatre we left.
Lovers had laughed at being sad
And justice, mercy were bereft
Of all abstractions. So were we,
Talking so low yet passionately.

CREATORS IN VIENNA

That dance we have heard of, so far back now that
We do not know who first pushed it gently into
A child's mind. But Vienna, Vienna, no mere tapping
In rooms or pavements. Ideas were dancing also, especially in
Four men's minds, ideas to change us, linking and breaking
Like dancers. The other two, a painter, a philosopher.
Four kings crowned now by decades of acceptance,

Two trying to heal—Freud, Adler leaping down our
Apparently never-before-discovered minds, entering our dreams,
Telling us of love and power, changing love and power,
And Kokoschka painting and enriching, purifying, disclosing,
Wittgenstein quietly challenging centuries of speculation.
                                        They are moving, moving still
These men, they pursue us. Time out of mind we
Check them, deny. As we do so they smile at us because

Our queries continually prove them right, their power
Is no Prospero-wand. They have discarded nothing at all
For our minds are brimmed with their voices, our hearts
Dance differently now. We are spellbound. We are islands.
Madness has been given order, painting pours out on posterity.
The thinker, as always, is pressed dry between two pages somewhere
Of a book containing the world, a book which can never be written.

ORPHEUS

Not looking back, not looking back—
For him that was the test. We have,
   All of us, camped out, somewhere, some time
In a place, underground or in full sunlight,
   Where we must choose. So our myths later
Instruct us, and our beliefs, whether in Eden
   Or oblivion, take for granted free-will,
Act on that assumption, even in unbelieving.

Thus Orpheus running through Hades with
A lyre so enchantable once, was himself
   Now enchained. That girl, she must, could be his.
But he must not look back. He saw light,
   A little like Lazarus, with the same trust,
The same astonishment, but for him life was behind
   In that place there. Misjudging the threshold
Or perhaps forgetting the promise, he turned, stunned,
   Seeing only darkness, no lyre could call her back, the girl
Had gone, the gods dealt out their punishment.

PERSEPHONE

For Spring and Summer she appeared and was
Blinded at first by light. To us she meant
Autumn and Winter were away because
For those two seasons she retreated, went

Back to the dark world, darker than our own.
When she arrived the petals opened to
Welcome her with their wreaths, twine round her throne.
Birds hatched their eggs and all things richly grew.

She went away quite silently one night.
The air was cold next day. From every tree
Leaves fell in dusty disarray to light
And burn the shadow of Persephone.

SNAKE CHARMER

The body writhes and rounds. The fingers feel
A circle, find a note. Up from the ground
Rears the caught serpent. It unwinds its coil
And dances to the sound

The player blows. His eyes address those eyes.
He is the choreographer who's made
The pattern of the dance, its length and size.
Danger is what is played.

In jeopardy, in thrall, the watchers can't
Help moving to the creature which they fear.
But they are safe as long as music's sent
Though that's not what they hear.

This is a rite but this is power also.
It happens now, yet enterprises such
As this take timid men to long ago
When the first reed's first touch

Haunted a jungle, hypnotised a snake.
This is no charming, this is courage when
At any moment faulty notes can break
Out anarchy again.

THE MINOTAUR

Daedalus designed this. Famous for buildings he did Minos' will.
Minos, full of revenge, yet could not
Kill this creature begotten by his wife and a bull coupling.
Poseidon punished him in this way,
Making for us a pattern as perfect and intricate as that labyrinth.
We want the danger, the escape, above all
We want a happy love story to cancel a passion which was prodigal
only of
A half-bull. Ariadne waited on this, patient as Penelope. She had seen
the handsome Athenians one by one
Go into Daedalus' design and die there. But she possessed joyfully the
power of a thread and a secret.

At first sight, as even classical writers will show and allow us, she
fell in love with Theseus who arrived
Apparently just a victim. But she, and we want this too, always this
necessity and ceremony,
Gave him the thread, the clue, the condition to be his wife. Theseus,
quick with courage and passion,
Took the twine from her, smiled and walked into the darkness
watchfully but fearlessly and found
The Minotaur sleeping. Beautiful indeed but now to be beaten to
death by young fists, exalted
In no bull-ring with panoply but providing us with the desired peril
before love suceeds,
Leading us gently into labyrinths within us where half-bulls
sometimes wake in our own darkness
And where we must always all be both Theseus and Ariadne.

NOT ABSTRACT

Where the river bends, where the bridges break,
Where the willow does not quite
Fall to the current—here is the place to stake
Your life in, your delight
Once easily lost. Here again you could make
A day out of half a night.

The moon is assured. The sun has put its back
Against the wood, the trees
Carry their rotten fruit like a swollen sack.
Stand among all of these
And learn from desertion and luxurious lack
Why some fall on their knees.

Gods have given. Gods have taken away
But left us with the need,
In angry arguments, logics which pray
Even for ghosts of a creed.
The bridge is broken and the willows sway.
Where does the river lead?

LITTLE PEACE

Through intricacy of sharp air
The urgent messages are sent.
Voices become a thoroughfare,
Crunched leaves are now irrelevant.

For seasons have resigned to let
Emergencies take on the sway
Where rules and governments once met
And legal systems drew each day

A quiet map, imposed a scheme
For living through. Now to exist
Through hours that shake men from a dream
Makes them take care not to be missed.

For not appearing will put them
In cells unwardered and unbarred.
Strange that a child still shouts its game
And has not heard the times are hard.

Trees shake, leaves drop. But who will win
Such trembling apprehensions warred
Where blood runs cold, blood-sheds begin,
That child ignoring and ignored?

Because huge violence is a threat,
A few are frenzied to be kind,
Warm one another yet, and yet
Hope is still hunted. Who will find?

57

SPY

The cleaving currents of dispute
Hold back. The vengeances now lie
With a few batteries of loot,
While a consenting, unhelped spy

Is wary, wondering what to do.
There may be armistice. He does
Not know the false reports from true
But waits in hiding. Is his cause

Or what he thought a war proclaimed
Ended? How long can he last out,
Starving now simply to be named,
Despair itself a thread of doubt?

PRISONER

Feel up the walls, waters ooze. The cold
Cranes down the spine. The wayward sky won't fit
A window, a square, but a square equates itself
With the eye in the brain, in the nervous system. All
Which flesh becomes without food and a little water.

I am tired. The planet curves, I cannot sleep.
How many moons have shone in how many shapes?
I am wistful in wisdom, honest in rich endearments,
Hollow perhaps, a channel for any whisper.
The long night takes my loneliness into its hands.

BEHIND ALL IRON CURTAINS

Ambassadors were dignified and curt
And even whispered in brocaded halls.
The slightest emphasis made someone start.
Meanwhile, pent anger hid behind the walls.

Answers were easy. It was questions which
Sent the eyes darting and the eyelids down.
One secretary slipped out of this reach,
Preferring all the tumult of the town.

Two wanted to make love but could not find
A room, a park, even a pool of shadow.
There was a haunting in the loving mind
And every mother seemed to be a widow.

One boy went out alone. There was a hush
Of people disappearing, then, far-off
A better tone, the beating, tidal rush.

He stood as though a statue in a hot
Strewn-with-siesta square. He heard a cough.
Smiling, he turned and, with a smile, was shot.

HAPPENINGS

Some say contentious Summers drove them to
A mountain range where they could touch the ice.
Then feel the finger-tip of thawing twice
When the hot cities cried "Our need is you."

Others were stunned awake, their mouths were sand
Choking, their spread of skin felt like a shore
Whose sweat was tides which only can withdraw.
They woke from this to lineaments of land.

And a forsaken few, who found forsaking
A suffering that pleased them with its skill,
Worked out proud plots their dreams could not fulfil
Though the beginnings had been so breath-taking.

Some kindly quiet ones were swept away
Until their own compassion cried "Be mild."
Madness caught up and set a mask that smiled
On such domestic, dutiful dismay.

Twelve great imaginations disappeared
Till someone's memory went deeply down
And grasped a goodness which they gave a crown.
Part of the world for two hours was not feared.

Visions and revolutions such as these
Are trusted to no treasure-hunts but lie
Beneath an unportending birdless sky
Waiting for, O, what men, what histories?

NOT FOR USE

A little of Summer spilled over, ran
In splashes of gold on geometry slates.
The grass unstiffened to pressure of sun.
I looked at the melting gates

Where icicles dropped a twinkling rain,
Clusters of shining in early December,
Each window a flaring, effulgent stain.
And easy now to remember

The world's for delight and each of us
Is a joy whether in or out of love.
"No one must ever be used for use,"
Was what I was thinking of.

WISHES

I hired a boat and told the sailors to
Take me to a hot island where the palms
Give you warm breath, and on the sands a few
Shells wait to be wrapped up in the sea's arms.

I begged a lonely man to show me where
A desert and a mirage might be found
And some oasis would give quenching air
As water blossomed from the ancient ground.

I asked some lovers if they knew the way
To some old friends of mine. They did not know;
They had not even heard the time of day.
The sunlight seemed to make their bodies glow.

I asked a priest where he had found his God.
He handed me a musty-smelling book.
I stared into his eyes and thought it odd
That he should have such an untrustful look.

I asked a child if he could cross the road
Safely. He did not speak but took my hand.
The shaking traffic seemed to shift my load
But there were thoughts I longed to understand.

ENDS

A city afraid of its darknesses,
Stone and wood and creeper wore
Their fitful mourning. An odd or even
Light appealed with a tiny gesture.
People ashamed of the cold they hide.

It could be the end of the world. It could
Be the almost last moment. Yes, there might
Have been a warning, men given a chance
To collect together their better feelings,
Create a contrition just in time.

We did not think it would be like this.
We imagined thunder-bolts or a blaze
Of all the stars colliding and clinging,
The moon head on to the sun. And so
It well may be. This is not the end.

In spite of the shame, in face of the fear
Half a cleaned Classical column withstood
The thriving moon which must increase.
Marching clouds were packing the sky
And one or two or three stepped clear.

PARTICULAR

Milk is on rocks, sea is only
Faintly tidal. The same sail draws
Its red sheet on a washing blue.
A telescope picks out rocks.
Limpets cling to their fastness.

Somebody's photograph? It wasn't.
Geologist's playground? No.
A scene unglossed by sentiment.
No one has ever been there.

A slice of an island this is.
The hem of a dream held fast.
Immaculate invitation.
A move towards innocence.

A place revered so richly
Is untampered as the moon.
But idylls are earmarked always
And we have set our seal

On the power which pulls a particular
Sea. This fragment of shore
Was sand-castled once by a child
But isn't now any more.

CHILDHOOD IN LINCOLNSHIRE

Six years of a flat land.
Grasses cut your fingers on that shore.
People kept calling it Holland and a child
Thought this on some map somewhere
Linked it with that place
A Dutch doll came from.
So the sea trafficked with imagination
Which was more luminous even
Than the blazing tulips in formidable ranks
Or honeysuckle,
The first flower to be seen and smelt,
Tied to its own event and potent for that, therefore, always.

LOSING AND FINDING

You had been searching quietly through the house
That late afternoon, Easter Saturday,
And a good day to be out of doors. But no,
I was reading in a north room. You knocked
On my door once only, despite the dark green notice,
"Do not disturb". I went at once and found you,

Paler than usual, not smiling. You just said
"I've lost them". That went a long way back
To running, screaming through a shop and knocking
Against giants. "I haven't had lunch", you said.
I hadn't much food and the shop was closed for Easter
But I found two apples and washed them both for you.

Then we went across the road, not hand in hand.
I was wary of that. You might have hated it
And anyway you were talking and I told you
About the river not far off, how some people
Swam there on a day like this. And how good the grass
Smelt as we walked to the Recreation Ground.

You were lively now as I spun you lying flat,
Talking fast when I pushed you on the swing,
Bold on the chute but obedient when, to your question
About walking up without hands, I said "Don't. You'll fall".
I kept thinking of your being lost, not crying,
But the sense of loss ran through me all the time

You were chatting away. I wanted to keep you safe,
Not know fear, be curious, love people
As you showed me when you jumped on my lap one evening,
Hugged me and kissed me hard. I could not keep you
Like that, contained in your joy, showing your need
As I wished *I* could. There was something elegiac

Simply because this whole thing was direct,
Chance, too, that you had found me when your parents
So strangely disappeared. There was enchantment
In the emptiness of that playground so you could
Be free for two hours only, noted by me, not you.
An Easter Saturday almost gone astray

Because you were lost and only six years' old.
And it was you who rescued me, you know.
Among the swings, the meadow and the river,
You took me out of time, rubbed off on me
What it feels like to care without restriction,
To trust and never think of a betrayal.

AN EVENT

Legs in knee-socks,
Standing on the rough playground,
Suddenly thinking, "Why am I here?"

No one else seemed near you,
Though they had been, still were
Except for this awareness.

Long before adolescence
This happened, happened more than once.
Is this the onset

Of that long-travelling,
Never answered
Question, "Who am I?"

It could be.
The state does not last
But the memory does.

And soon the shouts surround you again.
You have a blue and a red marble in your hand.
It is your turn to roll one.

USAGE

Creature-comforts other people call them
And what do they mean, just what precisely?
  One would gladly starve for weeks to have
That picture pinned up always, while another
  Would buy a toy rather than think of bread rolls.
And what exactly are these creatures, are they
  Listed in books of mammals? Are they insects?

  Birds possibly, the ones who loot a nest
Of one more bright than they. I am amazed
  When I discern the different ways we live,
Tastes we provide for, that we can have in common
  The same five senses and yet still allow,
In these at least, no singularity,
  While creature-comforts thrive upon their vagueness.

A THIRD

It was not that I intercepted
A look of love, as though trapped between two portraits.
I could have shared that, been included
Simply by recognising what I have seen directed
At me, a look so humanly open that a human being
Cannot bear it long and casts down his eyes.

No, this was altogether different, important
Only because it embarrassed, because it showed the
Gulfs and gaps between three people, also the tributaries
Linking them and separating them. What I saw
Was desire, something which cannot be shared,
Which twists you away not in wonder but horror.

Horror because one human being is appearing
Too appropriately like an animal, the other attempting
To change the look with a smile of longing acknowledged
Publicly. Better surely, to pair off under dark trees than
Confiscate, however briefly, the equal friendship of a third person.

NEED

Only you would notice what lay under
The practised smile, the just not jumping nerve.
You would have known this was a hint of thunder
To break out later. Yes, you would observe

The manners learnt yet meaning nothing now
But "Let's pretend." You've seen my nursery,
Sifted the pleasure from the grief, shown how

I need not act. The irony, you know,
Is when I'm with you I enjoy the part
Of playing someone else, put selves on show

Simply because I need not. I don't fit
Either the worn-out or the tempted heart.
Tell me the words to feel the truth of it.

ACCEPTED

You are no longer young,
Nor are you very old.
There are homes where those belong.
You know you do not fit
When you observe the cold
Stares of the old who sit

In bath-chairs or the park
(A stick, then, at their side),
Or find yourself in the dark
And see the lovers who,
In love and in their stride,
Don't even notice you.

This is a time to begin
Your life. It could be new.
The sheer not fitting in
With the old who envy you
And the young who want to win,
Not knowing false from true,

Means you have liberty
Denied to their extremes.
At last now you can be
What the old cannot recall
And the young long for in dreams,
Yet still include them all.

AN ABANDONED PALACE

A palace where the courtiers have vanished fleetly because
The work was too hard, and where they squabbled continually about
their rights
And the Queen's debt to them—this has foundered as if the close sea had
Rolled over and entered the doors. People ran out screaming.
Two stayed—an old woman bound to rheumatic fingers and the now
hard
Embroidery she insisted on finishing. The other was the undeposed but
rejected and
Uncomplaining Queen, who did not mind that the crown was covered
With mildew, the jewels were sold. She was subdued into a soft, slow,
Ever-expanding melancholy, though her eyes smiled,
Bidding farewell to the servants gone, asking only that
The steward should remain, add up the valuables and
Sell them. Then, in the high bedroom, she sat thinking

Of utter simplicities, the heir who had gone to travel the world and
had not
Written. In her note-book she wrote two words only, two words
Of disfigured defiance meaning almost total loss. The words were
"Find me." Quickly she took a moulting carrier pigeon to trust this
message to
And, with careful hands, glided the bird out of the tarnished windows
and then
Sat, waiting, occasionally visiting the trembling old woman, admiring
The progress of the stitching, herself hiding tears, still, somehow,
hoping for
Rescue, reprieve, an escape from a palace now a prison where hope itself
Taunted her continually with its expert disappointments,
Its refusal to gaze back at her long, caught in its own desperate incapacity.

74

RATHER LIKE A PEACOCK

You say you saw a bird much like a peacock,
Not proud of its own plumage, powerless with it
And being like a beacon to all comers,
Bedraggled birds, small but with the sharp
Anger and strength that comes when brightness is

Discerned, observed as dangerous, a threat
Simply by being passively attractive.
Yes, but among that gathering of birds,
Helpless, you said it was, and vulnerable.
Beaks bit into the colours and you thought

Of other creatures, human beings who
Have gifts not so flamboyant yet observed,
Envied. Tormentors, tireless as those birds,
Sense there's a threat, that here is something which
Might change their lives if given freedom, so,

They, who are quick at this thing only, find
The weak spot and with hostile words and looks
Darken that dazzle, rid themselves of fear
By forcing it upon the one they won't
Dare let it bring its brilliance to their minds.

What happened to that bird within your garden,
Target upon your turf? Could you scare off
Those small attackers, or were you too late?
Can you suggest a safe place for the being
Harassed just here, alive, alert, laid open?

GIVEN NOTICE
(for Clare)

It was the going back which gathered
A pack of thoughts, feelings also.
They spilt from my hands as I looked about.
A window which held contentment once
Framed a sky unfit for viewing,
But the grey of it fell with glare enough

On squat chessmen, a kaleidoscope,
A Russian bear, an Italian mug.
The full and flare of the place were rich,
But I in the middle of it was mute
Begging within myself for one,

Yes just one day and a different sky.
How hot I became with remembrances,
Then a feather of fear with strength enough
To connect the subtle silences,
Unhoard discourses valued now.

The room was an animal money-box
Smashed in pieces, the coins thrown down.
It was that returning which did it all,
Unlodged the losses I'd thought well-hidden—
People who came or did not come,

The bird outside which seemed to stick
On a single branch through a keepsake June
Of pell-mell skies and unscathed stars,
Broken yet holding petals and leaves,
All too much outside and within.

You who had never been before
Watched my wistfulness, saw the shrug,
Contained the sigh in a silence shared.
Toys are terrible, rooms are let
As blood is sometimes, for transfusion.

76

LEAVING A ROOM

Somebody said "Like an amputation,"
Another, "Part of your character."
Both were right: growing and breaking,
The nine, nineteen, nine hundred lives
Have been breathed in minutes, hours and weeks here,
Eighteen months by the calendar.
I have put both anchor and roots down.

My seasons were torn off a Summer layered
With raiding sunsets; bonfires blew
Away before me. Pictures faded
Slightly. I bronzed, slightly also.
What a litter of life I have crowded here,
What a residue of authentic gold!
I cannot keep it now.

The gallery, toyshop, study stand.
Clocks are striking round me, pendula
Pursue their energy. I have collected
Stars from that sky, laid them on ledges,
Rubbed shoulders with storms, the glass protecting.
Possessive, feverish, populous, I
Have plaited birds with their sounds. Today

Is not in time, is another order.
Nostalgia echoes, the early hours
Which were not hours are holding me.
I am tied up fast by trails of cards,
The threads of unfinished conversation.
I am a shape, a cube perhaps,
Now being sucked. But apparitions

Install themselves. I did not know
How acutely reliant I could be
On the lean of a card, the look of a toy.
Someone is taking over already.
Bruised by a fleck of dust, I pick
Some papers up and close my eyes

77

To the stars once fixed for me outside,
Stuff my ears against the insistent
Lovable echoes. I need a conversion,
Change into one who does not own,
Believe my belongings supply no need,
Then am heretic to the bone.

DEAF

Her mind is pushing slowly through the doors
Which others do not think about since they
Toss up their senses like a conjurer's
Five cards or streamers. She must find a way
To catch a tone or pause.

But it is nonsense that the eyes make up
For lack of hearing. Hers, obliquely bright,
Have no exchange with touch or tongue or lip.
Their brown is but a tension, not a sight,
But when the eyelids droop

She hunts and stalks her family. Their names
Come out in questions. Silver deaf-aid is
A mockery, a shaken box of themes
Whose high notes are distorted, dissonance,
As though she spoke her dreams

And asked us for the meaning. Hidden mind,
Muffled behind a face which never has
Tautened to adult enterprise, been lined
With cross-hatched disapprovals, your distress
Is terribly unblind.

NIGHT WORKER BY NATURE

Almost the last thing I shall see,
My morning is near waking time
For others. Factory night-workers
Are yawning at conveyor-belts,
   Newspapers fell off trains

Four hours ago. My lean-to hours,
Shaped small by others, not by me,
Are shuffled books, precluding lamp,
A curtain keeping out the stars.
   No stars, though, when I switch

The light off. One long strip of grey,
Where curtains can't be dragged to meet,
I watch, then hump my back against
Sky coming in to spark my feet,
   Sun-rise, two hours away.

Birds call across my almost-sleep,
Draw drowsy waking into my
Drowsing-asleep. Night-worker, I
Have felt reluctant power keep
   Clocks back but not that sky.

The only chanticleer I know
Runs with the wind, washed by the moon.
Its plumage folds. This cock has no
Voice to attend the day. The sun
   May gild it upon show.

I shall not see. My room takes form—
A Cubist's gathering of things
In muted colours, my last sight,
My dream-connected lingerings,
   My last touch on the night.

AN ATTEMPT TO CHARM SLEEP

A certain blue
A very dark one
Navy-blue
Going to school
Get back to colour
A pale blue
Somebody's eyes
Or were they grey
Who was the person
Did they like me
Go back to colour
An intolerant blue
A very deep
Inviting water
Is it a river
Where is it going
Shall I swim
What is its name
Go back to colour
Go back to waking
The spell doesn't work
As I stare at the night
It seems like blue.

THE POEM AT TIMES

Summons on the mind,
Seizing and questing, an
Attack, a coming to,
Excitement eased at once,
The found word, and the shine

As if, from water plucked
But never losing light,
Wash of the river still
Yet now on land at last.
The writing's on a spool.

BOX-ROOM

It is empty. Anyone entering hears
The creak of themselves. Boxes once
Held moth-eaten clothes and Teddy Bears.
That was before the going,
The gathering-up for the dance.

It is almost impossible to feel
Untouched by haphazard memory's glance.
Either your own or another's will steal
Into the gala of going,
The drawing-away to dance.

CANCER

Were the others warned of this also
Who saw the fingers flimsy as that disc
Of palatable bread, the over-flow
Of soda-water swallowed with no risk?
They must have seen the slow

Faltering, the body drooping dress
And cardigan. But they had their own ways—
Deafness, the tilted mind, or loneliness.
At first it was an ectoplasmic haze
I saw her through, distress,

Fear of my own, all that I had been told.
Motives don't mean much when uncoffined death
Walks in a woman not aware of cold,
Knowing, however, that each push of breath
Has not the power to hold.

She talked no stoic talk, nor thrived on past
Promise. She did not know I knew she had
The medical prediction and forecast—
A year or maybe two. Below my bed
She lies, but does she rest,

Does the Faith I was told of falter where
She is alone? She only let a hint
Of any creed out with a casual air,
Yes, almost an aside. Acceptance sent
Shivers through me, not her.

OBSERVING

That tree across the way
Has been a magnet to me all this year.
What happens to it is what interests me.
  I've watched a blackbird stay
Glued for a moment, unglue, disappear.
Violence came in April to that tree,
  Made its whole being sway

  Till I was sure it could
Not stand, would snap and in torn fragments lie,
Leaving another entrance for the sky.
  But that frail-seeming wood,
A conifer with intricate small leaves,
Stands under stars now while a new moon conceives
  Itself before the eye.

CELEBRATION OF WINTER

Any voice is soprano in this air,
Every star is seeding, every tree
Is a sign of belonging or being free,
Of being strong in the Winter atmosphere.
Nobody hesitates here.

There are sounds and there are spaces.
Human creatures could have left long ago,
Birds are migrants except
For an owl which woos and lullabies the night.
We are only waiting for snow.
The wind has swept away the brooding Summer,
Or has it taken flight?
Nostalgias are null. Eyes are a taper alight.

And Winter reaches ahead, it stretches, it goes
Further than dark. A fountain is somewhere still.
What voice will come and fill
The emptiness of its no-longer overflows?
Any birth in Winter is hallowed by more
Than Advents or Bethlehems. The seas compose
Themselves perhaps for an Age of Ice, a shore
Where a child lifts a wave, where one gull chose
Not an inland cluster but broken wing and claw.
Any voice is sharpened upon this air
And if the sky sagged there would be more than one star to spare.

TO GO WITH A PRESENT

I will risk threats of gazing at the most appetising
Mirrors and turning away with bleakness. I will gather more
    As a geologist than a gardener, stones where fossils may be engraved
And give you the completest. This will last and though lacking
    The bounty and exuberance of full Summer flowers
Be quiet as I wish, as I want these words to be. For gratitude

    Is an honour conferred and requires always that subtle
Blend of the spontaneous with the studied. With all thanks
    A present should go. You handed over more
Than a dedication. You gave me a portrait and a mood and I
    Am amazed still at the authority of your perception, your gentleness.

A LITTLE MORE

Each minute of a further light
Draws me towards perspective Spring.
I fold the minutes back each night,
    I hear the gossiping

Of birds whose instinct carries time,
A watch tucked in the flourished breast.
It ticks the second they must climb
    Into a narrow nest.

So birds. But I am not thus powered.
Impulse has gone. My measured cells
Of brain with knowledge are too stored,
    And trust to birds and bells.

Yet longer light is fetching me
To hopes I have no reason for.
A further lease of light each day
    Suggests irrational more.

COMFORT

Hand closed upon another, warm.
The other, cold, turned round and met
And found a weather made of calm.
So sadness goes, and so regret.

A touch, a magic in the hand.
Not what the fortune-teller sees
Or thinks that she can understand.
This warm hand binds but also frees.

THIS IS

This is to be unpossessive,
This is a way to earn
A portion of the clasp
Of sun. An eye can glean
The stars. They ride there still,
Are never gathered in.

And by nocturnal sea
A man may rest his dark
Which one wave laps upon.
This is a blessing, this
Awe which is silent, breath
Borne on a flight of wind.

NEVER GOING

We were always going
Further up the beach
Or further down,
However you regard it.
This was always planned
For after siesta
One afternoon,
But we never went.
Why didn't we?

Stopped by the heat?
More than once certainly.
Or was it the familiar walk
Where, even abroad,
We had made landmarks,
Wanted to stick to them,
Streets become personal
With our private names?

How easily then
We dismissed that journey
Thinking, I suppose,
"There will be another time.
Today is all wrong."
I shall not go there,
Not even to that town
Where you could have died.
No, that was elsewhere,
And that intended journey
Is prepared and plotted
For other people's footsteps.
There are no spoors of ours
And I won't go there alone.

May we retain
Such scope in which we play and love
    That we do not exclude
All those who have no heart to move,
    Fearing to spoil or strain,
Towards what is for us both joy and food.

    Abandon, then
Secret looks, I charge you, and
    This self I need to school
From subtle ways which guard a land
    And keep off other men.
This paradox will make us spare and full.

IN ITSELF

The rarity, the root, the flower,
The things themselves, not the abouts,
The magic wand of naming, power
That dreads away the darks, the doubts—

All this and see, a child appears
White as unfootstepped snow and strong
As dissipators of spread fears.
He stands and sings. It is a song

He's thought, a purpose of pure sound.
This child is conjurer, can make
The roots thrill in the frozen ground,
Petals fold up for buds to break.

GAINED

The day is not impoverished any more.
The sun came very late but never mind,
The sky has opened like an unwedged door
And for a moment we are all struck blind,
But blind with happiness. Birds' feathers toss
The air aside, regaining all the loss.

The loss of morning which was quietly grey,
Expectant, but what of? We did not know.
Our disappointment had discarded day
Until this early evening with its show
Of caught-up hours, sun's rising, sunset's glow.

PR6060
E52G7   **Jennings, Elizabeth, 1926-**
             Growing-points : new poems / by Elizabeth Jennings. —
             [Chester Springs, PA] Dufour Editions [c197
             94 p. ; 22 cm.   GB 75-09776
             ISBN 0-85635-122-9 :   ISBN 0-85635-123-7 pbk.

D43609

             I. Title.
             PR6060.E52G7   823'.9'14   75-318464
                                                                   MARC

             Library of Congress   75